Awesome ENDS IN ME

STAY FOCUSED.
KEEP CALM. BE POSITIVE.

AWESOME inc.®

A RESILIENCE & GRATITUDE JOURNAL FOR KIDS CREATED BY AWESOME INC

WWW.AWESOMEENDSIN.ME (NZ/AU)
WWW.THEAWESOMEINC.COM (USA)

DEDICATED TO
EMOTIONAL WARRIORS
EVERYWHERE

RESILIENT ME® GRATITUDE JOURNAL BY AWESOME INC®
BUILDING RESILIENCE & BOOSTING HAPPINESS

Content created by AwesoME Inc®
Cover design & typeset by Nicole Perry

Published by ME Incorporated Limited T/A AwesoME Inc®
PO Box 95158, Swanson, Auckland 0653, New Zealand

WWW.AWESOMEENDSIN.ME (NZ/AU)
WWW.THEAWESOMEINC.COM (USA)

I AM
Strong
UNIQUE
Precious
AMAZING
I AM Me

LEARN MORE ABOUT YOU AND WHAT MAKES YOU UNIQUE... BECAUSE YOU ARE AWESOME!

Growing up can be hard work! Sometimes we are happy and having fun, and at other times we are sad or angry, and sometimes we don't even know why. This journal will help you to get to know more about YOU, how your emotions work, how you can manage them, and how to use them wisely. You will learn what to do when life isn't going your way, and how to learn from mistakes, so you can live a happy and healthy life.

This journal is filled with easy activities to help you learn to build your resilience, boost your happiness, and improve your health and well-being, but most of all it is FUN!!

STAY FOCUSED. KEEP CALM. BE POSITIVE.

Sometimes it is easier to focus on what goes wrong in your life, or what you are not good at. But by focusing on those things it makes you feel like you aren't good enough, or that you don't have enough, or that only bad things happen to you. You can feel stressed and unhappy, even though there are a lot of positive things in your life. BUT did you know that you can rewire your brain to focus on the good things more! You can learn to think more clearly, and feel happier, and more content, more often. One of the absolute best ways to do this is by practising gratitude. **« AMAZING!**

On page 6 you will find out more about gratitude and the really cool ways it helps your brain and your body.

This journal will also show you how to focus on your strengths, help you flip your mood, create a positive attitude, use your energy for good and how to look after yourself plus awesome ways you can have fun with your friends and family. There are heaps of awesome things to fill in everyday so you can be happier and healthier. We hope you enjoy using it as much as we did creating it!

THE AWESOME INC® TEAM

ALL ABOUT ME...

NAME:

« THIS PERSON IS AMAZINGLY AWESOME!

AGE

FAVOURITE COLOUR

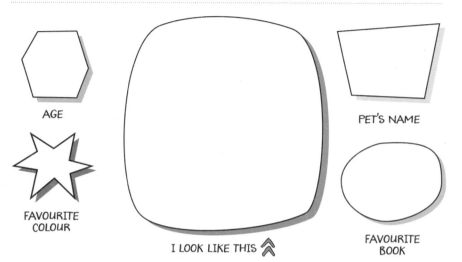

I LOOK LIKE THIS

PET'S NAME

FAVOURITE BOOK

MY FRIENDS ARE:

MY FAVOURITE THINGS TO DO:

WHAT IS GRATITUDE?

GRATITUDE IS THE EXPRESSION OF THANKFULNESS, OR APPRECIATION FOR SOMETHING YOU HAVE RECEIVED. BEING GRATEFUL ALLOWS YOU TO RECOGNISE AND ACKNOWLEDGE THE GOOD THINGS, PEOPLE, AND EVENTS IN YOUR LIFE.

OK, BUT WHY IS IT GOOD FOR ME?

1. **It FEELS good!** Gratitude is a positive emotion and when you experience a positive emotion the bliss or reward centre of your brain lights up. Cool, right!

2. **It improves your MOOD,** mental health and life satisfaction. Practicing gratitude helps to lessens the symptoms of anxiety and other negative emotions. It challenges your negative thought patterns, helping to calm you down and boost your mood.

3. **It helps you feel more CONNECTED.** When you recognise other people for what they do for you it helps to strengthen your relationship with them. You can feel greater connection and feel more satisfied with friends, family, school, community and yourself. It will help you feel more secure and valued by others.

4. **It increases your RESILIENCE.** Practising gratitude helps you bounce back from stressful events and helps you deal with tough times, by helping you to stop holding onto negative emotions.

5. **It improves your PHYSICAL HEALTH.** Practising gratitude strengthens your immune system, reduces the symptoms of illness, and helps to make you less bothered by aches and pains.

6. **It increases your ENGAGEMENT.** Practising gratitude makes you more generous and compassionate towards others, and helps keep you engaged in your schoolwork and hobbies, as well as making you less materialistic.

THINGS I AM GRATEFUL FOR ABOUT ME

THINGS I AM GRATEFUL TO HAVE IN MY LIFE

PEOPLE I AM GRATEFUL TO HAVE IN MY LIFE

SOMETIMES YOU TAKE FOR GRANTED WHAT REALLY MAKES YOU HAPPY. BY PRACTISING GRATITUDE YOU

>> STOP AND FOCUS ON THE GOOD STUFF <<

IN YOUR LIFE, WHICH HELPS YOU TO SEE MORE OF THE GOOD, LEAVING NO ROOM FOR THE NEGATIVE STUFF.

HOW TO PRACTICE GRATITUDE...

CHECK OUT THIS EXAMPLE >>

Just be thankful for your everyday life – your family, friends, your body, your school, your home, food, pets. Writing 3-4 times a week is the ideal amount.

Savour surprises. Record events that were awesome, unexpected or surprising. Or be grateful for times you avoided something bad happening.

Keep the negative out. Be positive and focus on the good! Your brain has a weird way of focusing on the negative, for example instead of saying " I am grateful that I didn't miss the bus this morning." try " I am grateful that I was early for the bus this morning."

Think of what things allow you to do or feel. Legs help you to run, bed makes you feel safe, Mum makes you feel loved, your bike takes you places.

Focus on people.
Recognise when they intentionally give up something to help you, like time or energy, and think about the benefit of that to you.

Consider life without. Try imagining what your life would be like without certain people or things, write down how they help you.

Count your gifts. Thinking of the good things in your life as gifts helps you to not take them for granted. Try to relish and savor the gifts you've received.

Revise and repeat. If you find yourself writing the same things that is OK but try to hone in on a different detail each time.

It is the simple things in life that can really make you feel happy, if you stop and notice.

21/2/19

DATE

I can do anything I put my mind to.

TODAY I AM GRATEFUL FOR:

My legs because they are strong
and help me to run fast.
The SUN is shining and it makes
me feel happy!
I scored 2 goals this week
I am getting better with
practice every week.
MUM! She made my
favourite dinner YUM!
Thanks Mum.

MY HAPPINESS SCALE

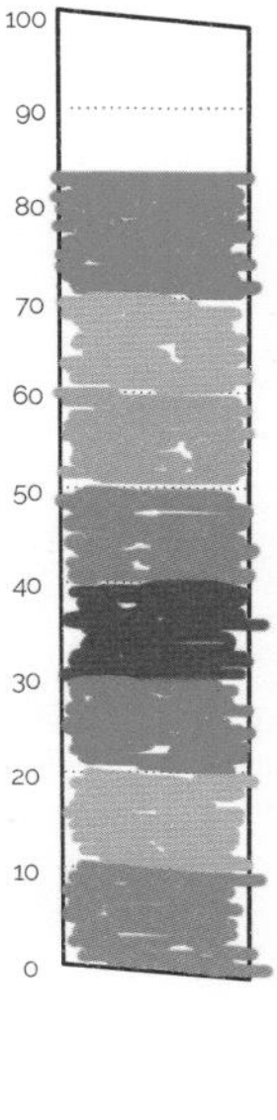

I AM FEELING:

THANK YOU FOR ALL THE AMAZING THINGS IN MY LIFE!

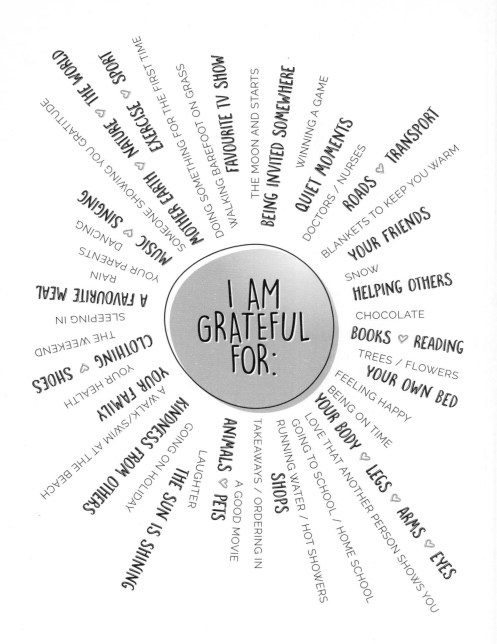

I AM GRATEFUL FOR:

- THE WORLD ♡ NATURE ♡ MOTHER EARTH
- SPORT ♡ EXERCISE
- DOING SOMETHING FOR THE FIRST TIME
- WALKING BAREFOOT ON GRASS
- FAVOURITE TV SHOW
- THE MOON AND STARTS
- BEING INVITED SOMEWHERE
- WINNING A GAME
- QUIET MOMENTS
- DOCTORS / NURSES
- ROADS ♡ TRANSPORT
- BLANKETS TO KEEP YOU WARM
- YOUR FRIENDS
- SNOW
- HELPING OTHERS
- CHOCOLATE
- BOOKS ♡ READING
- TREES / FLOWERS
- YOUR OWN BED
- FEELING HAPPY
- BEING ON TIME
- YOUR BODY ♡ LEGS ♡ ARMS ♡ EYES
- LOVE THAT ANOTHER PERSON SHOWS YOU
- GOING TO SCHOOL / HOME SCHOOL
- RUNNING WATER / HOT SHOWERS
- SHOPS
- TAKEAWAYS / ORDERING IN
- A GOOD MOVIE
- ANIMALS ♡ PETS
- LAUGHTER
- THE SUN IS SHINING
- GOING ON HOLIDAY
- KINDNESS FROM OTHERS
- A WALK/SWIM AT THE BEACH
- YOUR FAMILY
- YOUR HEALTH
- CLOTHING ♡ SHOES
- THE WEEKEND
- SLEEPING IN
- A FAVOURITE MEAL
- RAIN
- YOUR PARENTS
- DANCING
- MUSIC ♡ SINGING
- SOMEONE SHOWING YOU GRATITUDE

IF YOU GET STUCK ON THINGS TO BE GRATEFUL FOR
USE THESE EXAMPLES FOR INSPIRATION

NOW YOUR TURN! »

/ /

DATE

Every day is a fresh start.

TODAY I AM GRATEFUL FOR:

SOMETHING I LEARNED TODAY:

MY HAPPINESS SCALE

100
90
80
70
60
50
40
30
20
10
0

I AM FEELING:

ANGRY SAD OK HAPPY EXCITED SILLY

THANK YOU FOR ALL THE AMAZING THINGS IN MY LIFE!

/ /

DATE

TODAY I AM GRATEFUL FOR:

MY HAPPINESS SCALE

100
90
80
70
60
50
40
30
20
10
0

THE BEST PART OF TODAY WAS:

THANK YOU FOR ALL THE AMAZING THINGS IN MY LIFE!

I AM FEELING:

ANGRY SAD OK HAPPY EXCITED SILLY

/ /

DATE

I choose to be happy.

TODAY I AM GRATEFUL FOR:

MY HAPPINESS SCALE

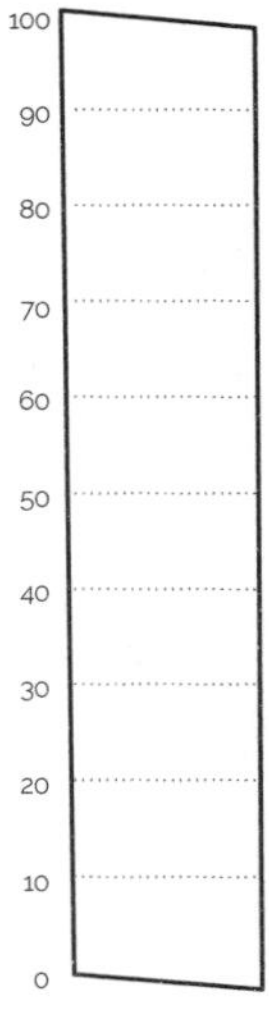

I AM FEELING:

ANGRY SAD OK HAPPY EXCITED SILLY

THANK YOU FOR ALL THE AMAZING THINGS IN MY LIFE!

I stand for what is right.

/ /

DATE

SOMETHING AWESOME THAT HAPPENED:

TODAY I AM GRATEFUL FOR:

MY HAPPINESS SCALE

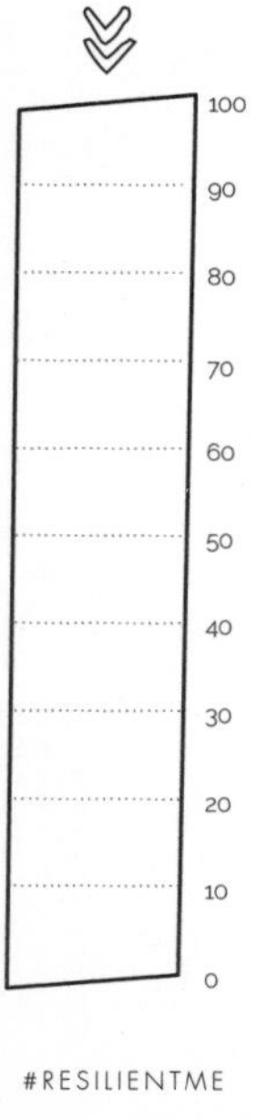

THANK YOU FOR ALL THE AMAZING THINGS IN MY LIFE!

I AM FEELING:

/ /

DATE

I am confident in who I am.

TODAY I AM GRATEFUL FOR:

SOMETHING I LEARNED TODAY:

MY HAPPINESS SCALE

100
90
80
70
60
50
40
30
20
10
0

I AM FEELING:

ANGRY SAD OK HAPPY EXCITED SILLY

THANK YOU FOR ALL THE AMAZING THINGS IN MY LIFE!

I believe in me.

/ /

DATE

TODAY I AM GRATEFUL FOR:

MY HAPPINESS SCALE

100
90
80
70
60
50
40
30
20
10
0

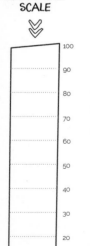

THANK YOU FOR ALL THE AMAZING THINGS IN MY LIFE!

I AM FEELING:

ANGRY SAD OK HAPPY EXCITED SILLY

/ /

DATE

I learn from my mistakes.

TODAY I AM GRATEFUL FOR:

MY HAPPINESS SCALE

100
90
80
70
60
50
40
30
20
10
0

I AM FEELING:

ANGRY SAD OK HAPPY EXCITED SILLY

THANK YOU FOR ALL THE AMAZING THINGS IN MY LIFE!

WHAT MAKES ME AWESOME?

Fill in your answers:

I am unique because...
I am most happy when I am...
I am confident when...
I am proud of myself when I...
My favourite skill is...
When I grow up I want to be...
I am ME

COME BACK TO THESE PAGES AS A QUICK REMINDER WHEN YOU ARE FEELING SAD.

NICE THINGS MY FRIENDS SAY ABOUT ME

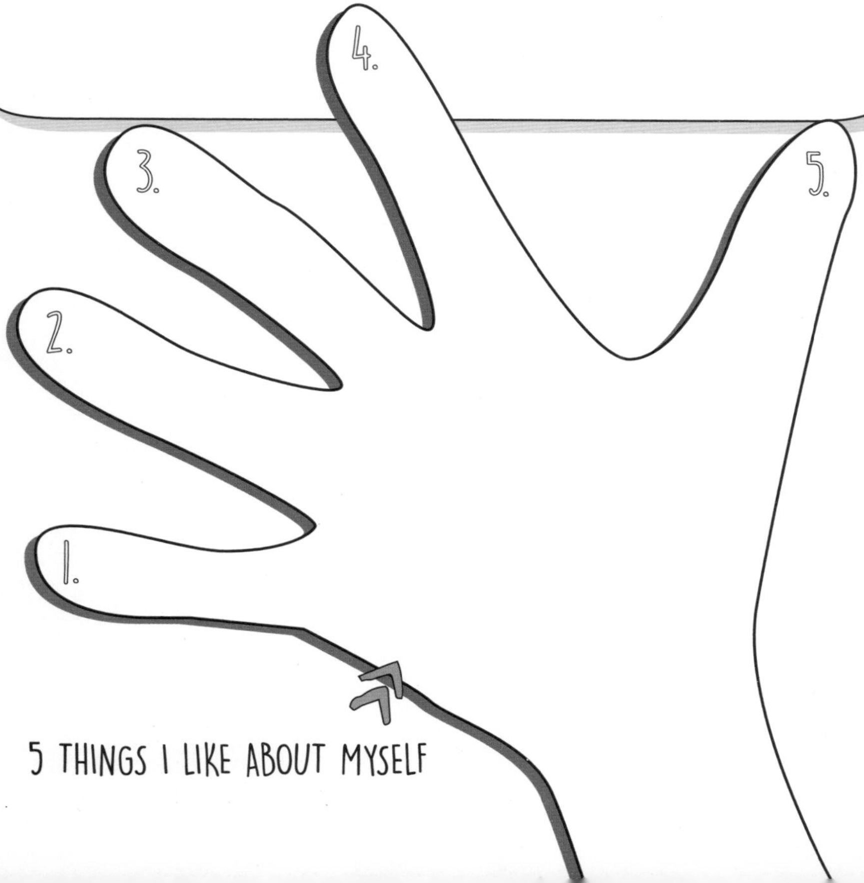

5 THINGS I LIKE ABOUT MYSELF

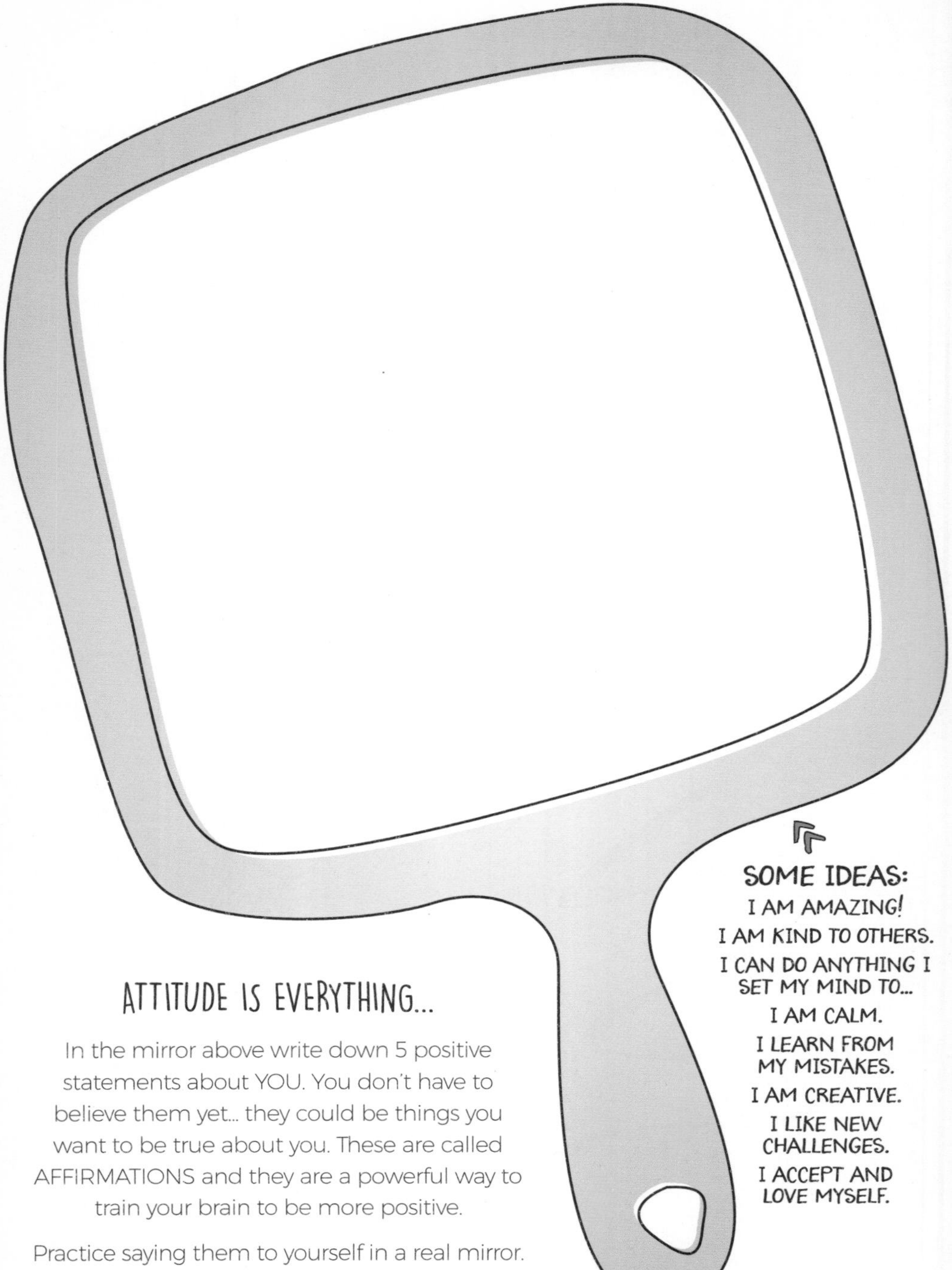

ATTITUDE IS EVERYTHING...

In the mirror above write down 5 positive statements about YOU. You don't have to believe them yet... they could be things you want to be true about you. These are called AFFIRMATIONS and they are a powerful way to train your brain to be more positive.

Practice saying them to yourself in a real mirror.

SOME IDEAS:

I AM AMAZING!

I AM KIND TO OTHERS.

I CAN DO ANYTHING I SET MY MIND TO...

I AM CALM.

I LEARN FROM MY MISTAKES.

I AM CREATIVE.

I LIKE NEW CHALLENGES.

I ACCEPT AND LOVE MYSELF.

WHAT ARE MY STRENGTHS?

By learning how to focus on what you do well, or are good at – called your strengths – instead of focusing on what you don't do well, you can learn to be resourceful, and build your resilience. Your strengths don't mean how fast you can run, how high you can climb, or how well you play computer games....

YOUR STRENGTHS ARE WHAT COMES NATURALLY TO YOU, THAT YOU DO EASILY, OR WHAT EXCITES AND MOTIVATES YOU.

WHAT COMES NATURALLY TO ME?

e.g. helping others,
playing rugby,
being positive...

GUESS WHAT!
YOU'VE ALREADY WRITTEN YOUR STRENGTHS ON THE PREVIOUS PAGES!! GO BACK AND HAVE A LOOK AGAIN.

A SUBJECT I'M CONFIDENT TO TALK ABOUT

I COMPARE MYSELF TO OTHER PEOPLE:

- [ ] I do this all the time!
- [ ] I sometimes do.
- [ ] I never do.

FOCUS ON WHAT YOU ARE GOOD AT!
NOTICING WHAT YOU DO WELL HELPS YOU TO FOCUS LESS ON WHAT DOESN'T COME NATURALLY, AND YOU STOP COMPARING YOURSELF TO OTHERS.

CHALLENGE NEGATIVE THOUGHTS

When you want to learn or try something new do you tell yourself all kinds of negative stuff like you are not smart enough, or good enough? Or think you won't be able to do, so you don't even try...

THIS IS CALLED A FIXED MINDSET.

I'M GOING TO FAIL AND GET LAUGHED AT.
I'M JUST GOING TO GIVE UP.
I ALWAYS MAKE MISTAKES!
IT'S NO USE TRYING.
I WILL NEVER LEARN HOW TO DO THIS.
I'LL NEVER BE AS GOOD AS MY FRIENDS!

BUT DID YOU KNOW...
You can learn to quiet or turn that voice down by focusing on your strengths and your positive qualities. You can approach new and challenging tasks with the view that you just don't know how to do them YET. Rather than you can't do it at all. It is called having a **GROWTH MINDSET.**

Challenging negative thoughts with a growth mindset means you:

Know you can get better by working hard.

Keep trying when you fail or when things get tough.

Learn from feedback or criticism.

Put in effort and practice.

Embrace challenges.

Learn from your mistakes.

Try different ways to find a solution to your problem.

DON'T GIVE UP!

PRACTICE BEING POSITIVE WITH A
GROWTH MINDSET

Practice saying these examples to yourself.

EFFORT MAKES ME STRONGER.
I CAN GET BETTER WITH PRACTICE.
I LIKE TO CHALLENGE MYSELF.
I ASK FOR HELP WHEN I NEED IT.
GETTING BETTER TAKES TIME.
I CAN LEARN HARD THINGS.
I'M ON THE RIGHT TRACK.
I WILL KEEP TRYING.
I WILL LEARN HOW TO DO THIS.
I CAN LEARN FROM MY MISTAKES!
I CAN'T DO IT YET!

Fill in your own examples in the blank bubbles.

REWARD YOURSELF FOR EFFORT.
BY TRYING YOU ARE LEARNING, AND PROBLEM SOLVING AND IT WILL MAKE YOU FEEL REALLY GOOD!

CHALLENGES

Help Me

To GROW

GROW YOUR MINDSET!

COME BACK TO THIS PAGE TO REMIND YOURSELF TO JUST KEEP TRYING.

SOME THINGS I'M NOT GOOD AT YET:

WHAT CAN I DO TO IMPROVE?

IF MY PLAN DOESN'T WORK, WHAT WILL I DO?

CHANGE YOUR PERSPECTIVE!

CHORES I DON'T MIND DOING

if your parents know you prefer some jobs over others, they might negotiate with you!

I choose my own attitude.

/ /

DATE

TODAY I AM GRATEFUL FOR:

MY HAPPINESS SCALE

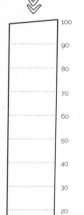

100
90
80
70
60
50
40
30
20
10
0

THANK YOU FOR ALL THE AMAZING THINGS IN MY LIFE!

I AM FEELING:

ANGRY SAD OK HAPPY EXCITED SILLY

/ /

DATE

I get better every single day.

TODAY I AM GRATEFUL FOR:

MY HAPPINESS SCALE

100
90
80
70
60
50
40
30
20
10
0

I AM FEELING:

ANGRY SAD OK HAPPY EXCITED SILLY

THANK YOU FOR ALL THE AMAZING THINGS IN MY LIFE!

Today is going to be amazing.

/ /
DATE

TODAY I AM GRATEFUL FOR:

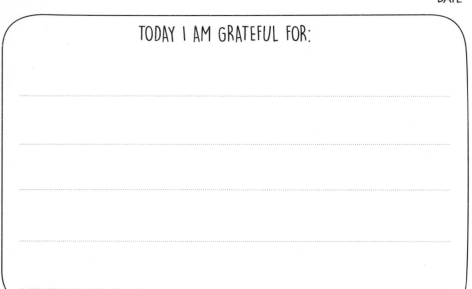

MY HAPPINESS SCALE

100
90
80
70
60
50
40
30
20
10
0

THE BEST PART OF TODAY WAS:

THANK YOU FOR ALL THE AMAZING THINGS IN MY LIFE!

I AM FEELING:

ANGRY SAD OK HAPPY EXCITED SILLY

/ /

DATE

I show others I care.

WHAT I DID WELL TODAY:

TODAY I AM GRATEFUL FOR:

MY HAPPINESS SCALE

100
90
80
70
60
50
40
30
20
10
0

I AM FEELING:

ANGRY SAD OK HAPPY EXCITED SILLY

THANK YOU FOR ALL THE AMAZING THINGS IN MY LIFE!

I am a great listener.

/ /

DATE

TODAY I AM GRATEFUL FOR:

MY HAPPINESS SCALE

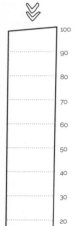

100
90
80
70
60
50
40
30
20
10
0

THANK YOU FOR ALL THE AMAZING THINGS IN MY LIFE!

I AM FEELING:

ANGRY SAD OK HAPPY EXCITED SILLY

/ /

DATE

I like myself the way I am.

TODAY I AM GRATEFUL FOR:

MY HAPPINESS SCALE

100
90
80
70
60
50
40
30
20
10
0

I AM FEELING:

ANGRY SAD OK HAPPY EXCITED SILLY

THANK YOU FOR ALL THE AMAZING THINGS IN MY LIFE!

I am beautiful inside and out.

/ /

DATE

SOMETHING AWESOME THAT HAPPENED:

TODAY I AM GRATEFUL FOR:

MY HAPPINESS SCALE

100
90
80
70
60
50
40
30
20
10
0

THANK YOU FOR ALL THE AMAZING THINGS IN MY LIFE!

I AM FEELING:

ANGRY SAD OK HAPPY EXCITED SILLY

MY

Attitude

IS MINE

TO

Choose

UNDERSTANDING EMOTIONS

Every one feels and experiences a whole range of emotions, like happiness, sadness, anxiety, anger, excitement, fear and joy. Remember that ALL EMOTIONS ARE NORMAL, even the negative ones, that are often the hardest to deal with.

Understanding and accepting your emotions will help you to control them. Next time you feel a big emotion try these steps. You will need to practice this when you feel calm.

1. What emotion are you feeling? Can you name it?

2. Now say its name out loud, or in your head. Notice how it is affecting you. Are you crying? Are you clenching your fists or talking quickly?

3. Take a deep breath and tell yourself it will pass, like a cloud passing overhead, or water running over your skin.

COLOUR IN SOME EMOTIONS YOU HAVE FELT RECENTLY:

SADNESS

Includes
GRIEF, DEPRESSION, and LONELINESS

You can get sad for lots of reasons like: you made a mistake, you feel left out, someone you love goes away or you got hurt.

Sometimes you don't even know why you feel sad! But that is OK. Every one feels sad sometimes, and like all emotions it will pass.

FEAR

Includes ANXIETY, WORRY and TERROR.

Fear is a reaction to when you feel threatened, or powerless. It is a vital physical response that evolved from when we needed to protect ourselves from predators! You might not be chased by wild animals anymore but your brain still treats threats as life or death.

TRY THIS TIP!!

When feeling anxious or scared instead of trying to calm yourself down by saying things like: *"I am not worried"* try saying *"I am excited!"*

Anxiety and excitement make your body react in the same way – racing heart beat, sweating - so it is an easier jump from anxious to excited, than from anxious to calm. So STOP fighting against your emotions, just embrace and accept them. Change your focus from what could go wrong to what could go right. **Focus on the good!**

EMOTIONS ARE NOT "GOOD" OR "BAD".

ALL EMOTIONS ARE NORMAL! WE NEED A WIDE RANGE OF EMOTIONS TO LIVE A HEALTHY LIFE!

ANGER

Includes FRUSTRATION, RAGE and IRRITATION.

Anger can be felt on many levels. You can react this way if you feel threatened, or you can get angry if you feel you aren't treated fairly, if you are critisised or if you want something you can't have. It is all part of being human. Anger can even be good sometimes because it helps you to stand up for what you believe in. It can also be a response to not knowing how to handle other emotions.

It's OK to have negative emotions and it's OK to cry... Sometimes letting your tears flow makes you feel better, and helps get the emotion out. If you feel sad all the time talk to someone you trust about it.

DID YOU KNOW... WE LEARN TO MIRROR EMOTIONS WHEN WE ARE BABIES? IT HELPS US TO UNDERSTAND THEM BY COPYING THE PEOPLE AROUND US.

GUESS THE EMOTION...

Pair up with your brother, sister or a friend, sit opposite each other, one person starts making faces that correspond to an emotion below, while the other person tries to guess which emotion they are displaying.

Tick off the ones you guess correct.

- ☐ angry
- ☐ surprised
- ☐ disappointed
- ☐ bored
- ☐ happy
- ☐ guilty
- ☐ confused
- ☐ sad
- ☐ excited
- ☐ hurt
- ☐ nervous
- ☐ jealous
- ☐ scared
- ☐ disgusted
- ☐ embarrassed
- ☐ amused

FLIP YOUR MOOD...

THERE ARE MANY DIFFERENT WAYS YOU CAN HELP MANAGE NEGATIVE EMOTIONS, SO THEY DON'T LINGER AROUND FOR LONG.

TRY THESE IF YOU ARE FEELING IT HARD TO FLIP THAT NEGATIVE ENERGY:

RUN AROUND OR JUMP ON A TRAMPOLINE - Exercising releases some chemicals in your brain and body that help you feel great.

DO SOMETHING KIND FOR SOMEONE ELSE – This will help you to stop worrying about you and focus on someone else. See page 67 for ideas.

TALK TO SOMEONE – Telling people how you feel can make you feel better. If you feel sad but not sure why, just say"I feel sad and I don't know why."

GET INTO NATURE – go for a walk outside, climb or sit under a tree. You don't need to talk, just surround yourself in the beauty of nature.

GRATITUDE! Write what you are grateful for in this journal. Think about all the things that are wonderful in your life. For inspiration check out the gratitude list on page 10.

YOU CAN USE THESE METHODS IF YOU ARE FEELING ANGRY, SCARED, GUILTY, WORRIED OR ANXIOUS.

SOMETIMES ONE THING WILL WORK, SOMETIMES YOU NEED TO DO MORE THAN ONE THING TO FLIP YOUR MOOD.... DON'T GIVE UP!

DISTRACTION – Try and do something else to take your mind off things. Try some colouring in, dance around the room to your favourite song, or take a bath.

BREATHING – Take some deep breaths right down into your belly while counting to four in your head. See page 62.

Remember:

I am in charge of my emotions!

WHAT CAN I DO TO FLIP MY MOOD?

1.

2.

3.

WHAT MAKES ME HAPPY?

REMEMBER: IT'S NOT POSSIBLE TO BE HAPPY ALL THE TIME! AND THAT'S OK!!!!!

USE SOME WORDS TO DESCRIBE WHAT MAKES YOU HAPPY.

Come back to this page when you are feeling sad, for ideas on flipping your mood.

HAPPINESS includes LOVE, JOY and PEACE.

Happiness is our natural state, you can be happy when you are playing with your friends, spending time with family, or just knowing you have a lot to be thankful for.

Happiness is considered a positive emotion because it makes you feel good inside.

WHAT IS THE NICEST THING SOMEONE HAS DONE FOR YOU?

WHAT MAKES YOUR FAMILY HAPPY?

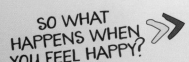

SO WHAT HAPPENS WHEN YOU FEEL HAPPY?

Your brain releases feel good chemicals when something makes you happy. Little messengers then send signals to other parts of your body, so your heart might race, you sweat, get butterflies in your tummy or you might even cry!

WHEN YOU ARE FEELING SAD, USE THESE IDEAS FOR SOME SELF-CARE.

25 WAYS TO LOOK AFTER YOU

- SIT IN NATURE
- HAVE SOME DEVICE FREE TIME
- DANCE LIKE NO-ONE IS WATCHING
- MAKE YOUR BED
- TAKE A SHOWER OR BATH
- WALK BAREFOOT ON THE GRASS
- READ A BOOK
- TALK TO A FRIEND
- HAVE A HEALTHY SNACK
- WRITE IN THIS JOURNAL
- DO SOMETHING NEW
- CLIMB A TREE
- GO FOR A RUN
- GO FOR A WALK
- SIT IN THE SUN
- VISUALISE SOMETHING AWESOME
- LISTEN TO MUSIC
- CHANGE YOUR ENVIRONMENT
- HUG A PET
- TAKE SOME DEEP BELLY BREATHS
- DO SOME COLOURING IN
- WATCH SOMETHING FUNNY
- DO SOME MEDITATION
- LAY ON YOUR BACK AND WATCH THE CLOUDS
- DO SOMETHING NICE FOR SOMEONE

/ /

DATE

I can do whatever I focus my mind on.

TODAY I AM GRATEFUL FOR:

MY HAPPINESS SCALE

100
90
80
70
60
50
40
30
20
10
0

I AM FEELING:

ANGRY SAD OK HAPPY EXCITED SILLY

THANK YOU FOR ALL THE AMAZING THINGS IN MY LIFE!

I enjoy learning about new things.

/ /

DATE

TODAY I AM GRATEFUL FOR:

THE BEST PART OF TODAY WAS:

MY HAPPINESS SCALE

100
90
80
70
60
50
40
30
20
10
0

THANK YOU FOR ALL THE AMAZING THINGS IN MY LIFE!

I AM FEELING:

ANGRY SAD OK HAPPY EXCITED SILLY

/ /

DATE

I love and accept myself.

WHAT I DID WELL TODAY:

TODAY I AM GRATEFUL FOR:

MY HAPPINESS SCALE

100
90
80
70
60
50
40
30
20
10
0

I AM FEELING:

ANGRY SAD OK HAPPY EXCITED SILLY

THANK YOU FOR ALL THE AMAZING THINGS IN MY LIFE!

I take care of my body.

/ /

DATE

TODAY I AM GRATEFUL FOR:

MY HAPPINESS SCALE

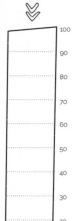

100
90
80
70
60
50
40
30
20
10
0

THANK YOU FOR ALL THE AMAZING THINGS IN MY LIFE!

I AM FEELING:

ANGRY SAD OK HAPPY EXCITED SILLY

/ /
DATE

I have special gifts and talents.

TODAY I AM GRATEFUL FOR:

SOMETHING I LEARNED TODAY:

MY HAPPINESS SCALE

100 90 80 70 60 50 40 30 20 10 0

I AM FEELING:

ANGRY SAD OK HAPPY EXCITED SILLY

THANK YOU FOR ALL THE AMAZING THINGS IN MY LIFE!

Learning is fun and exciting.

/ /

DATE

SOMETHING AWESOME THAT HAPPENED:

TODAY I AM GRATEFUL FOR:

MY HAPPINESS SCALE

100
90
80
70
60
50
40
30
20
10
0

THANK YOU FOR ALL THE AMAZING THINGS IN MY LIFE!

I AM FEELING:

ANGRY SAD OK HAPPY EXCITED SILLY

DATE / /

I improve with lots of practice.

TODAY I AM GRATEFUL FOR:

MY HAPPINESS SCALE

100
90
80
70
60
50
40
30
20
10
0

I AM FEELING:

ANGRY SAD OK HAPPY EXCITED SILLY

THANK YOU FOR ALL THE AMAZING THINGS IN MY LIFE!

I am a problem solver.

/ /

DATE

TODAY I AM GRATEFUL FOR:

MY HAPPINESS SCALE

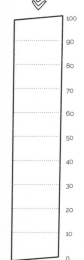

100
90
80
70
60
50
40
30
20
10
0

THE BEST PART OF TODAY WAS:

THANK YOU FOR ALL THE AMAZING THINGS IN MY LIFE!

I AM FEELING:

ANGRY SAD OK HAPPY EXCITED SILLY

/ /

DATE

I go after my dreams.

TODAY I AM GRATEFUL FOR:

MY HAPPINESS SCALE

100
90
80
70
60
50
40
30
20
10
0

I AM FEELING:

ANGRY SAD OK HAPPY EXCITED SILLY

THANK YOU FOR ALL THE AMAZING THINGS IN MY LIFE!

I won't give up.

/ /

DATE

TODAY I AM GRATEFUL FOR:

THE BEST PART OF TODAY WAS:

MY HAPPINESS SCALE

100
90
80
70
60
50
40
30
20
10
0

THANK YOU FOR ALL THE AMAZING THINGS IN MY LIFE!

I AM FEELING:

ANGRY SAD OK HAPPY EXCITED SILLY

DATE / /

I am important in this world.

WHAT I DID WELL TODAY:

TODAY I AM GRATEFUL FOR:

MY HAPPINESS SCALE

100
90
80
70
60
50
40
30
20
10
0

I AM FEELING:

ANGRY SAD OK HAPPY EXCITED SILLY

THANK YOU FOR ALL THE AMAZING THINGS IN MY LIFE!

I am free to be myself.

/ /

DATE

TODAY I AM GRATEFUL FOR:

MY HAPPINESS SCALE

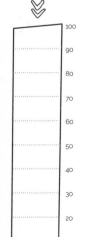

100
90
80
70
60
50
40
30
20
10
0

THANK YOU FOR ALL THE AMAZING THINGS IN MY LIFE!

I AM FEELING:

ANGRY SAD OK HAPPY EXCITED SILLY

/ /

DATE

I see beauty all around me.

TODAY I AM GRATEFUL FOR:

MY HAPPINESS SCALE

100
90
80
70
60
50
40
30
20
10
0

I AM FEELING:

ANGRY SAD OK HAPPY EXCITED SILLY

THANK YOU FOR ALL THE AMAZING THINGS IN MY LIFE!

I make others feel good about themselves.

/ /

DATE

SOMETHING AWESOME THAT HAPPENED:

TODAY I AM GRATEFUL FOR:

MY HAPPINESS SCALE

100
90
80
70
60
50
40
30
20
10
0

THANK YOU FOR ALL THE AMAZING THINGS IN MY LIFE!

I AM FEELING:

ANGRY SAD OK HAPPY EXCITED SILLY

DATE / /

I am honest.

TODAY I AM GRATEFUL FOR:

SOMETHING I LEARNED TODAY:

MY HAPPINESS SCALE

100
90
80
70
60
50
40
30
20
10
0

I AM FEELING:

ANGRY SAD OK HAPPY EXCITED SILLY

THANK YOU FOR ALL THE AMAZING THINGS IN MY LIFE!

Kindness is my superpower.

/ /

DATE

TODAY I AM GRATEFUL FOR:

MY HAPPINESS SCALE

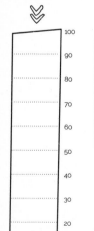

100
90
80
70
60
50
40
30
20
10
0

THANK YOU FOR ALL THE AMAZING THINGS IN MY LIFE!

I AM FEELING:

ANGRY SAD OK HAPPY EXCITED SILLY

/ /

DATE

I'm getting stronger every day.

WHAT I DID WELL TODAY:

TODAY I AM GRATEFUL FOR:

MY HAPPINESS SCALE

100
90
80
70
60
50
40
30
20
10
0

I AM FEELING:

ANGRY SAD OK HAPPY EXCITED SILLY

THANK YOU FOR ALL THE AMAZING THINGS IN MY LIFE!

I am fearless.

/ /

DATE

TODAY I AM GRATEFUL FOR:

THE BEST PART OF TODAY WAS:

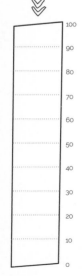

MY HAPPINESS SCALE

100
90
80
70
60
50
40
30
20
10
0

THANK YOU FOR ALL THE AMAZING THINGS IN MY LIFE!

I AM FEELING:

ANGRY SAD OK HAPPY EXCITED SILLY

/ /

DATE

I can share my talents with others.

TODAY I AM GRATEFUL FOR:

MY HAPPINESS SCALE

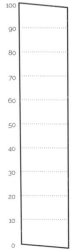

100
90
80
70
60
50
40
30
20
10
0

I AM FEELING:

ANGRY SAD OK HAPPY EXCITED SILLY

THANK YOU FOR ALL THE AMAZING THINGS IN MY LIFE!

I know my worth.

/ /

DATE

TODAY I AM GRATEFUL FOR:

MY HAPPINESS SCALE

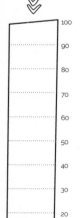

100
90
80
70
60
50
40
30
20
10
0

THANK YOU FOR ALL THE AMAZING THINGS IN MY LIFE!

I AM FEELING:

ANGRY SAD OK HAPPY EXCITED SILLY

I Will Do
MY BEST
AND That IS
Always
Enough

STAY CALM WITH BELLY BREATHING

THIS IS A SUPER EASY WAY YOU CAN TAKE BACK CONTROL OF YOUR EMOTIONS WHEN YOU FEEL UPSET, SCARED OR ANXIOUS.

Learning to concentrate on your breath, and breathe deep into your belly, helps to slow down your heart rate, and relax your muscles, so you can stay calm and focus.

1. Sit up straight and place your hands on your tummy OR lay down on the floor and place a soft toy, or hands, on your belly. You may also like to close your eyes.

2. Breathe in through your nose, imagine you are smelling a flower, and count to 4 in your head. Make sure to breathe all the way into your belly. You will feel your tummy rise underneath your hand or toy.

3. Hold your breath for one count.

4. Now breathe out through your mouth, imagine you are blowing out a candle, while counting to 4. Feel all the air empty out of your tummy.

5. Repeat at least 5 times.

IF YOUR MIND WANDERS DON'T GIVE UP! JUST BRING YOUR THOUGHTS BACK TO YOUR BREATHING.
PUPPIES ARE CUTE!
I'M HUNGRY!

TOP TIP...
MAKE SURE TO PRACTICE WHEN YOU ALREADY FEEL CALM SO YOU CAN USE IT WHEN YOU REALLY NEED IT.

GRATITUDE IS YOUR SECRET WEAPON

When you are using your deep breathing try focusing on the area around your heart, while also thinking about something or someone you really love and appreciate.

STEP 1.

Focus on your heart. Imagine your breath is flowing in and out through your heart or chest area, breathing a little slower and deeper than usual right into your belly.

STEP 2.

Remember a time you felt really good inside - laughing with friends, a special hug with someone you love, a special place you visited. Go back there in your mind and try to re-imagine that feeling.

HOW DOES IT WORK...

BY recreating this feeling you are activating a big nerve that runs up the centre of your body. We like to call the feeling a WARM FUZZY. By doing this your heart works in sync with your brain and it STOPS stress in its tracks!

SOME MORE IDEAS TO CALM YOURSELF DOWN

- HUG A TREE
- LIE ON YOUR BACK WITH YOUR FEET UP A WALL
- LIE ON YOUR BACK ON THE GRASS AND WATCH THE CLOUDS
- BEND OVER TO TOUCH YOUR TOES AND COUNT TO 5
- GO FOR A WALK
- PAINTING
- COLOURING IN
- TAKE A BATH
- COUNT BACKWARDS FROM 100
- SHAKE A GLITTER JAR SEE HOW TO MAKE ONE ON THE NEXT PAGE

DESCRIBE A TIME YOU FELT REALLY GOOD INSIDE

Where were you, who were you with, what were you doing? Think of it next time you do your belly breathing.

STOP!
QUIET YOUR MIND

ENGAGE YOUR FIVE SENSES, CLOSE YOUR EYES, BREATHE DEEPLY AND PAY ATTENTION TO RIGHT NOW...

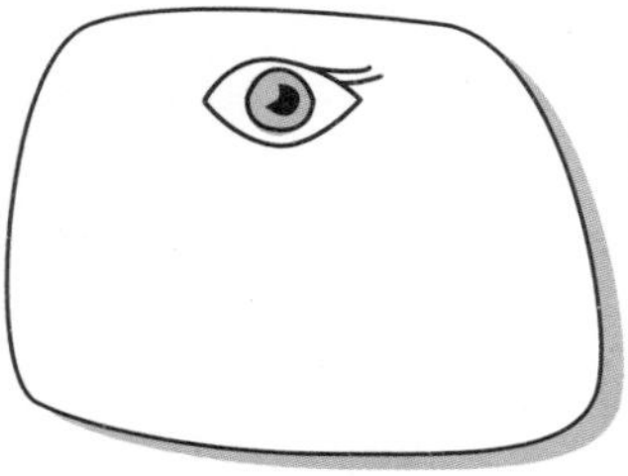

WHAT CAN YOU SEE?

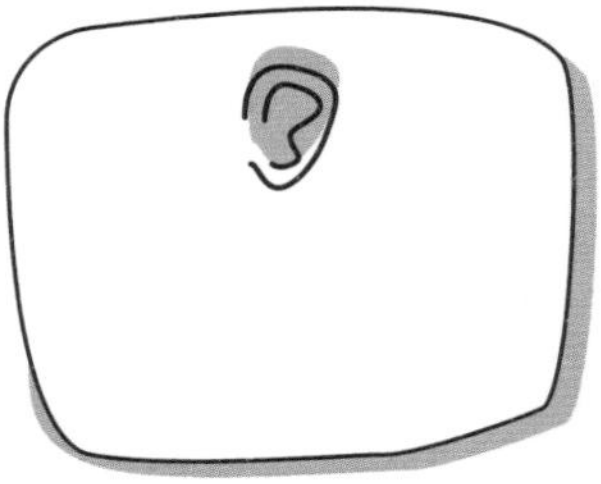

WHAT CAN YOU HEAR?

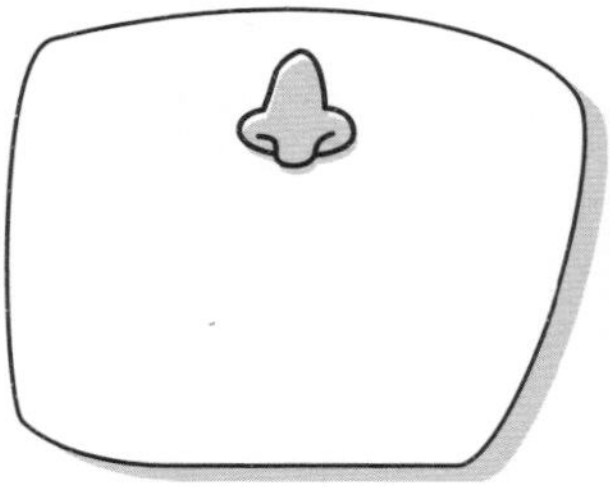

WHAT CAN YOU SMELL?

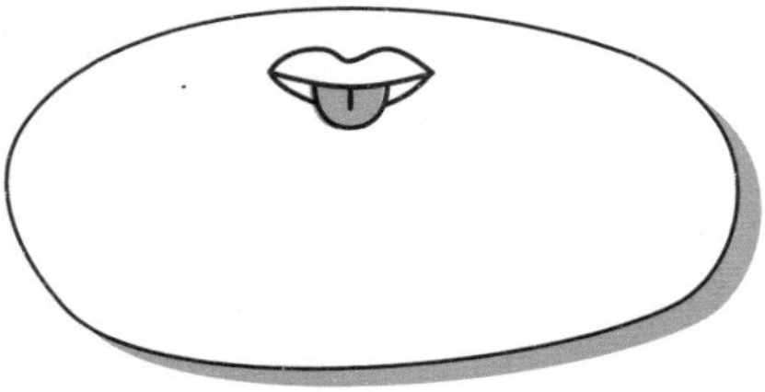

WHAT CAN YOU TASTE?

WHAT CAN YOU FEEL?

THIS IS CALLED MINDFULNESS AND IS A TYPE OF MEDITATION.

Stop and take notice of the things you usually take for granted, while also paying close attention to your breathing, and accept what you are feeling. It will help you to manage your emotions and help you to feel more in control.

THE COOLEST THING ABOUT MINDFULNESS IS YOU CAN DO IT ANYWHERE!!!

MAKE MINDFULNESS A HABIT

PRACTISING MINDFULNESS CAN HELP MAKE YOU HAPPIER AND HELP TO LESSEN FEELINGS OF ANXIETY.

Remember if you are feeling frustrated or anxious to S.T.O.P.

Stop what you are doing. **T**ake a breath. **O**bserve and acknowledge what is happening - inside and outside of you - and **P**roceed what you were doing after checking in with yourself.

YOU CAN MAKE THIS AND USE IT WHEN YOU FEEL UPSET

MAKE A GLITTER JAR

YOU WILL NEED:
A JAR WITH A LID, WATER, RUNNY GLUE AND GLITTER.

STEP 1.
FILL YOUR JAR WITH WATER.

STEP 2.
ADD A BIG SPOON FULL OF RUNNY GLUE.

STEP 3.
ADD A BIG SPOON FULL OF GLITTER.

STEP 4.
PUT THE LID ON YOUR JAR AND SHAKE!

Watch the glitter swirl around when you shake the jar... this is what your mind is like when you are stressed, mad or upset.

The glitter is your thoughts... ALL OVER THE PLACE!

Now put the jar down and keep watching... the glitter starts to settle and the water clears. When you take a moment to be still, and breathe deep into your belly, your mind will do the same thing. Your thoughts will start to settle and you will see things much clearer.

KINDNESS IS MAGIC!

DID YOU KNOW WE ARE WIRED TO BE KIND?

When we are babies, and starting to engage more with the people around us, it is our natural instinct to be helpful to others. Have you ever noticed your baby brother, sister or cousin pick up something you have dropped, and hand it back to you?

But why do we do this without understanding why we do it? Because IT FEELS GOOD! Being kind, helpful and giving to others releases feel-good chemicals that activate the parts of our brains associated with trust, pleasure and connection. So it makes you feel happy!

KINDNESS IS CONTAGIOUS. WHEN YOU SEE SOMEONE DO SOMETHING KIND IT GIVES YOU THE SAME GOOD FEELING, SO MAKES YOU WANT TO DO IT TOO!

BEST OF ALL BEING KIND MAKES OTHER PEOPLE FEEL AMAZING TOO!!

The more you are kind the more you want to be kind. It trains your brain because you are rewarded with good feelings and 'warm fuzzies' in your heart. The trick is to do it without being asked.

THINGS I HAVE DONE TO BE KIND:

1.

2.

3.

BEING KIND MAKES ME FEEL...

35 ACTS OF

RANDOM KINDNESS

Here is a list of things you can do to be kind. Tick them off as you complete them.

DID YOU KNOW... SPENDING MONEY ON OTHER PEOPLE MAKES YOU FEEL HAPPIER THAN WHEN YOU SPEND IT ON YOURSELF?

- [ ] Pick up rubbish
- [ ] Say hello to everyone
- [ ] Smile at everyone
- [ ] Hold a door for someone
- [ ] Leave happy notes for people
- [ ] Compliment a friend
- [ ] Donate clothes that no longer fit you
- [ ] Set the table for dinner
- [ ] Make Mum/Dad a cup of tea
- [ ] Talk to someone new at school
- [ ] Invite someone to play
- [ ] Give your teacher flowers
- [ ] Write a poem for someone
- [ ] Send a letter to your grandparents
- [ ] Write a postcard to a friend
- [ ] Make a gift for someone
- [ ] Plant a tree
- [ ] Ask for donations instead of gifts on your birthday
- [ ] Do some baking for a neighbour
- [ ] Clean up without being asked
- [ ] Check in on an elderly neighbour
- [ ] Teach someone something new
- [ ] Help out in the garden
- [ ] Donate food to a charity
- [ ] Donate your pocket money to charity
- [ ] Write fun messages in chalk on the footpath to inspire others
- [ ] Make Mum breakfast in bed
- [ ] Donate toys to a kids charity
- [ ] Wash someones car
- [ ] Let someone go in front of you in line
- [ ] Help raise money for a good cause
- [ ] Do a favour without asking for anything in return
- [ ] Do you brothers/sisters chores for them
- [ ] Say something kind to yourself
- [ ] Write a letter of gratitude to someone

ADD SOME MORE OF YOUR OWN:

>> ....

....

....

....

THINK OF ALL THE GREAT PEOPLE AND GOOD THINGS IN YOUR LIFE, AND WHAT A HUGE DIFFERENCE THEY MAKE TO YOU EVERY DAY.

SAY THANK YOU

WRITE A LETTER OF GRATITUDE

Think of someone who has done something for you but you have never thanked. It could be a teacher, a friend, parent or coach? Write them a letter describing what they did for you, how it made you feel and why you are grateful to them. You don't need to send it for it to make you feel good, but imagine that person reading that letter, or better still – seeing them in person and reading it to them!

HAPPINESS TIP:

Say 'Thank you' as much as you can to as many people as you can. Thank them for the little things, like letting you in front of them in line, but also for the big stuff too, like your parents for caring for you. Not only will it make them feel happy but it will make you feel more positive emotions, relish good experiences, improve your health, plus help you deal with difficult situations and build stronger relationships with others.

Showing other people you are grateful to have them in your life will help you to feel more connected to them, and acknowledging what others do for you will help with your feelings of self-worth.

/ /

DATE

DEAR

I can do this!

/ /

DATE

TODAY I AM GRATEFUL FOR:

MY HAPPINESS SCALE

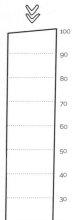

100
90
80
70
60
50
40
30
20
10
0

THANK YOU FOR ALL THE AMAZING THINGS IN MY LIFE!

I AM FEELING:

ANGRY SAD OK HAPPY EXCITED SILLY

DATE / /

I inspire others.

TODAY I AM GRATEFUL FOR:

SOMETHING I LEARNED TODAY:

MY HAPPINESS SCALE

100
90
80
70
60
50
40
30
20
10
0

I AM FEELING:

ANGRY SAD OK HAPPY EXCITED SILLY

THANK YOU FOR ALL THE AMAZING THINGS IN MY LIFE!

I use my failures as lessons.

/ /

DATE

SOMETHING AWESOME THAT HAPPENED:

TODAY I AM GRATEFUL FOR:

MY HAPPINESS SCALE

100
90
80
70
60
50
40
30
20
10
0

THANK YOU FOR ALL THE AMAZING THINGS IN MY LIFE!

I AM FEELING:

/ /

DATE

I am who I want to be.

TODAY I AM GRATEFUL FOR:

MY HAPPINESS SCALE

100
90
80
70
60
50
40
30
20
10
0

I AM FEELING:

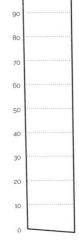

ANGRY SAD OK HAPPY EXCITED SILLY

THANK YOU FOR ALL THE AMAZING THINGS IN MY LIFE!

My mind is open to learning.

/ /
DATE

TODAY I AM GRATEFUL FOR:

THE BEST PART OF TODAY WAS:

MY HAPPINESS SCALE

100
90
80
70
60
50
40
30
20
10
0

THANK YOU FOR ALL THE AMAZING THINGS IN MY LIFE!

I AM FEELING:

ANGRY SAD OK HAPPY EXCITED SILLY

/ /

DATE

I love my body.

WHAT I DID WELL TODAY:

TODAY I AM GRATEFUL FOR:

MY HAPPINESS SCALE

100
90
80
70
60
50
40
30
20
10
0

I AM FEELING:

ANGRY SAD OK HAPPY EXCITED SILLY

THANK YOU FOR ALL THE AMAZING THINGS IN MY LIFE!

I am confident.

/ /
DATE

TODAY I AM GRATEFUL FOR:

MY HAPPINESS SCALE

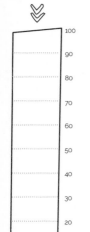

100
90
80
70
60
50
40
30
20
10
0

THANK YOU FOR ALL THE AMAZING THINGS IN MY LIFE!

I AM FEELING:

ANGRY SAD OK HAPPY EXCITED SILLY

/ /

DATE

I deserve good things to happen to me.

TODAY I AM GRATEFUL FOR:

MY HAPPINESS SCALE

100

90

80

70

60

50

40

30

20

10

0

I AM FEELING:

ANGRY SAD OK HAPPY EXCITED SILLY

THANK YOU FOR ALL THE AMAZING THINGS IN MY LIFE!

I am happy to be alive.

/ /

DATE

SOMETHING AWESOME THAT HAPPENED:

TODAY I AM GRATEFUL FOR:

MY HAPPINESS SCALE

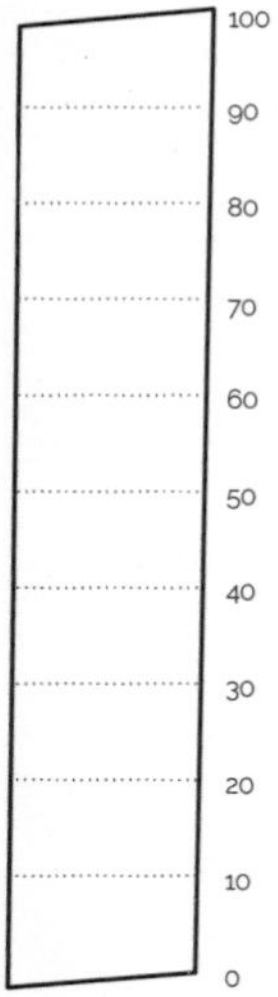

THANK YOU FOR ALL THE AMAZING THINGS IN MY LIFE!

I AM FEELING:

/ /
DATE

I know everything is possible.

TODAY I AM GRATEFUL FOR:

SOMETHING I LEARNED TODAY:

MY HAPPINESS SCALE

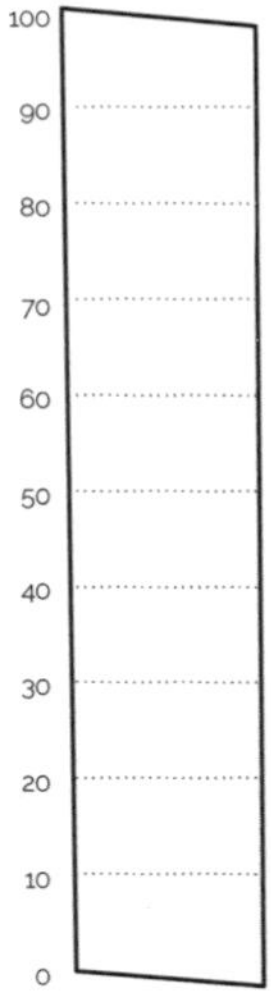

I AM FEELING:

ANGRY SAD OK HAPPY EXCITED SILLY

THANK YOU FOR ALL THE AMAZING THINGS IN MY LIFE!

I am unique and amazing.

/ /

DATE

TODAY I AM GRATEFUL FOR:

MY HAPPINESS SCALE

100
90
80
70
60
50
40
30
20
10
0

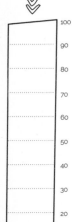

THANK YOU FOR ALL THE AMAZING THINGS IN MY LIFE!

I AM FEELING:

ANGRY SAD OK HAPPY EXCITED SILLY

/ /
DATE

I only compare myself to myself.

WHAT I DID WELL TODAY:

TODAY I AM GRATEFUL FOR:

MY HAPPINESS SCALE

100
90
80
70
60
50
40
30
20
10
0

I AM FEELING:

ANGRY SAD OK HAPPY EXCITED SILLY

THANK YOU FOR ALL THE AMAZING THINGS IN MY LIFE!

I believe in my goals and dreams.

/ /

DATE

TODAY I AM GRATEFUL FOR:

MY HAPPINESS SCALE

100
90
80
70
60
50
40
30
20
10
0

THANK YOU FOR ALL THE AMAZING THINGS IN MY LIFE!

I AM FEELING:

ANGRY SAD OK HAPPY EXCITED SILLY

STAY
Focused
KEEP CALM
BE
Positive

YOUR BRAIN LOVES EXERCISE

BY GETTING MORE MOVEMENT IN YOUR DAY YOU WILL BE...

✓ **HAPPIER** ✓ **ENERGISED** ✓ **MOTIVATED** ✓ **FOCUSED**

EXERCISE I LOVE TO DO:

- [ ] Riding my bike
- [ ] Running
- [ ] Soccer
- [ ] Rugby
- [ ] Netball
- [ ] Basketball
- [ ] Jumping/trampoline
- [ ] Climbing a tree
- [ ] Dancing
- [ ] Jumping waves
- [ ] Swimming
- [ ] Walking
- [ ] Tramping/Bush walking
- [ ] Playing tag
- [ ] Skipping/Jump rope
- [ ] Yoga
- [ ] Headstand
- [ ] Gymnastics
- [ ] Athletics
- [ ] Hula hooping
- [ ] Hopscotch
- [ ] Table tennis
- [ ] Triathlon
- [ ] Martial Arts

Add your own:

>>

<<

THE AIM IS TO GET YOUR HEART PUMPING!

Exercising regularly can give you an enormous sense of well-being. You will feel more energetic, sleep better, have a better memory, feel more relaxed and more positive about yourself and your life. PLUS it will make you feel strong!

EVEN A LITTLE BIT OF MOVEMENT IS BETTER THAN NOTHING! FOCUS ON AN ACTIVITY THAT YOU ENJOY, OR MAKE IT SOCIAL AND JOIN A TEAM SPORT WITH YOUR FRIENDS.

GET OUTSIDE and MOVE

HAPPINESS TIP:

Going for a walk outside, in the bush or at the beach, makes you feel more refreshed and energetic, and less tense and angry.

Exercise increases feel-good brain chemicals and reduces the level of stress hormones in your body. The mood benefits of just 20 minutes of exercise can last up to 12 hours.*

MOVING MY BODY MAKES ME FEEL...

REMEMBER THESE ACTIVITIES THAT MAKE YOU FEEL HAPPY AND ENERGISED. USE THEM WHEN YOU NEED TO FLIP YOUR MOOD.

Pay attention to how you feel next time you exercise.
Use words and pictures to describe your feelings.

*ACCORDING TO A 2013 STUDY PUBLISHED IN THE JOURNAL OF PSYCHOLOGY OF SPORT AND EXERCISE

FEED YOUR MIND

IF YOUR BRAIN DOESN'T GET THE RIGHT FUEL TO FUNCTION, IT CAN LEAVE YOU FEELING SAD, WORRIED OR WITH NO ENERGY.

Eating healthy foods that support your brain will also help you to feel good. If some types of food make you feel bloated, anxious, uncomfortable or sleepy then they are probably best avoided. You don't need to starve yourself just listen to your body and eat foods that make you feel energised and amazing.

HEALTHY EATING TIPS

EAT food that has the least amount of ingredients. Food with only one ingredient is often called wholefood... these include fruit, vegetables and meat.

NOTICE how you feel after you eat. If you feel energised and content that is good. If you feel bloated, gassy, or sick then that is not so good.

CREATE a vege garden, you may need some help with this, but try growing vegetables and herbs. Watch them grow, pick them and then eat them... you may be more likely to try them if you have grown them yourself.

TRY a new food as often as possible. You never know you might love it! Your tastebuds change as you get older so you might love some foods you used to hate.

CHOOSE a country and then either cook, or go out to try a meal from that country. The whole family can take turns to choose. It is a great way to try food you wouldn't normally eat.

HELP Mum or Dad with preparing your food - make sure to touch, smell and talk about the food, where it comes from, how it is made, and how it is cooked.

START YOUR MEALS WITH A MOMENT OF GRATITUDE

Give thanks for the food you get to eat, and for the person who prepared it for you.

REMEMBER... A LITTLE BIT OF 'JUNK' FOOD THAT YOU LOVE IS OK, JUST DON'T HAVE IT ALL THE TIME!

SOME FRUITS AND VEGETABLES I LIKE:

SOME FOOD I DON'T LIKE NOW, BUT I WILL TRY AGAIN:

Just like a race car you work better when you get the best quality fuel for your body.

FOOD THAT MAKES ME FEEL AMAZING

FOOD THAT MAKES ME FEEL YUCK!

TIME FOR LIGHTS OUT!

GOOD QUALITY SLEEP IS SO IMPORTANT FOR YOUR BODY AND MIND. Your body and your brain need deep rest to grow and develop, and good quality sleep helps you to stay strong and healthy. It helps you to think more clearly, to solve problems and concentrate better.

YOU NEED 10–12 HOURS SLEEP EACH NIGHT

On the first clock below mark what time you get up out of bed. Count back 12 hours and mark on the second clock what time you should be going to bed to get the right amount of sleep.

TIME YOU GET UP

TIME YOU NEED TO BE IN BED

WHAT HAPPENS WHEN YOU GET:

GOOD SLEEP

Better attention span

Better at problem solving

Better mood

Get on better with others

Healthier

BAD SLEEP

Forgetful

Moody

Grumpy

No energy

Can't concentrate

Irritated easily

Sick more often

YOU SHOULD AIM TO GO TO SLEEP AND WAKE UP AT THE SAME TIME EVERY DAY.

HOW TO GET THE BEST SLEEP

KEEP YOUR BEDROOM COOL, DARK AND AS QUIET AS POSSIBLE.

DON'T DRINK HIGH SUGAR DRINKS BEFORE BED.

AVOID BIG MEALS BEFORE BED.

KEEP SMART PHONES, TVS OR TABLETS OUT OF YOUR BEDROOM.

EXERCISE DURING THE DAY.

GET PLENTY OF NATURAL LIGHT EXPOSURE DURING THE DAY.

CREATE YOUR OWN CALMING BEDTIME ROUTINE.

CREATE YOUR OWN
BEDTIME ROUTINE

CREATE A SCHEDULE OF THE SAME RELAXING THINGS YOU CAN DO EACH NIGHT...

eg. shower or bath, brush your teeth, read a book, write in this journal, cuddles with mum or dad, do some mindfulness meditation or listen to calming music.

1.

2.

BY CREATING A REGULAR ROUTINE THAT CALMS YOU DOWN, YOUR BODY WILL LEARN THE SIGNALS FOR WHEN IT IS TIME TO GO TO SLEEP.

3.

4.

A GOOD NIGHTS SLEEP!

I am kind.

/ /

DATE

SOMETHING AWESOME THAT HAPPENED:

TODAY I AM GRATEFUL FOR:

MY HAPPINESS SCALE

100
90
80
70
60
50
40
30
20
10
0

THANK YOU FOR ALL THE AMAZING THINGS IN MY LIFE!

I AM FEELING:

ANGRY SAD OK HAPPY EXCITED SILLY

/ /

DATE

I love to listen.

TODAY I AM GRATEFUL FOR:

MY HAPPINESS SCALE

100
90
80
70
60
50
40
30
20
10
0

I AM FEELING:

THANK YOU FOR ALL THE AMAZING THINGS IN MY LIFE!

I am capable of so much.

/ /
DATE

TODAY I AM GRATEFUL FOR:

MY HAPPINESS SCALE

100
90
80
70
60
50
40
30
20
10
0

THANK YOU FOR ALL THE AMAZING THINGS IN MY LIFE!

I AM FEELING:

ANGRY SAD OK HAPPY EXCITED SILLY

/ /

DATE

It is OK to not know everything.

WHAT I DID WELL TODAY:

TODAY I AM GRATEFUL FOR:

MY HAPPINESS SCALE

100
90
80
70
60
50
40
30
20
10
0

I AM FEELING:

ANGRY SAD OK HAPPY EXCITED SILLY

THANK YOU FOR ALL THE AMAZING THINGS IN MY LIFE!

I can make a difference.

/ /

DATE

TODAY I AM GRATEFUL FOR:

MY HAPPINESS SCALE

100
90
80
70
60
50
40
30
20
10
0

THANK YOU FOR ALL THE AMAZING THINGS IN MY LIFE!

I AM FEELING:

ANGRY SAD OK HAPPY EXCITED SILLY

/ /

DATE

All of my problems have solutions.

TODAY I AM GRATEFUL FOR:

SOMETHING I LEARNED TODAY:

MY HAPPINESS SCALE

100
90
80
70
60
50
40
30
20
10
0

I AM FEELING:

ANGRY SAD OK HAPPY EXCITED SILLY

THANK YOU FOR ALL THE AMAZING THINGS IN MY LIFE!

I can be anything I want to be.

/ /

DATE

SOMETHING AWESOME THAT HAPPENED:

TODAY I AM GRATEFUL FOR:

MY HAPPINESS SCALE

100
90
80
70
60
50
40
30
20
10
0

THANK YOU FOR ALL THE AMAZING THINGS IN MY LIFE!

I AM FEELING:

/ /

DATE

It is enough to do my best.

TODAY I AM GRATEFUL FOR:

MY HAPPINESS SCALE

100
90
80
70
60
50
40
30
20
10
0

I AM FEELING:

ANGRY SAD OK HAPPY EXCITED SILLY

THANK YOU FOR ALL THE AMAZING THINGS IN MY LIFE!

I have everything I need right now.

/ /

DATE

TODAY I AM GRATEFUL FOR:

MY HAPPINESS SCALE

100
90
80
70
60
50
40
30
20
10
0

THE BEST PART OF TODAY WAS:

THANK YOU FOR ALL THE AMAZING THINGS IN MY LIFE!

I AM FEELING:

/ /

DATE

I can get through anything.

TODAY I AM GRATEFUL FOR:

SOMETHING I LEARNED TODAY:

MY HAPPINESS SCALE

100
90
80
70
60
50
40
30
20
10
0

I AM FEELING:

ANGRY SAD OK HAPPY EXCITED SILLY

THANK YOU FOR ALL THE AMAZING THINGS IN MY LIFE!

My positive thoughts create positive feelings.

/ /

DATE

SOMETHING AWESOME THAT HAPPENED:

TODAY I AM GRATEFUL FOR:

MY HAPPINESS SCALE

100
90
80
70
60
50
40
30
20
10
0

THANK YOU FOR ALL THE AMAZING THINGS IN MY LIFE!

I AM FEELING:

ANGRY SAD OK HAPPY EXCITED SILLY

/ /

DATE

I stand up for what I believe in.

TODAY I AM GRATEFUL FOR:

MY HAPPINESS SCALE

100
90
80
70
60
50
40
30
20
10
0

I AM FEELING:

ANGRY SAD OK HAPPY EXCITED SILLY

THANK YOU FOR ALL THE AMAZING THINGS IN MY LIFE!

Learning is fun and exciting.

/ /

DATE

TODAY I AM GRATEFUL FOR:

MY HAPPINESS SCALE

100
90
80
70
60
50
40
30
20
10
0

THANK YOU FOR ALL THE AMAZING THINGS IN MY LIFE!

I AM FEELING:

/ /

DATE

I can and I will!

WHAT I DID WELL TODAY:

TODAY I AM GRATEFUL FOR:

MY HAPPINESS SCALE

100
90
80
70
60
50
40
30
20
10
0

I AM FEELING:

ANGRY SAD OK HAPPY EXCITED SILLY

THANK YOU FOR ALL THE AMAZING THINGS IN MY LIFE!

My life is challenging and fun.

/ /

DATE

TODAY I AM GRATEFUL FOR:

MY HAPPINESS SCALE

100
90
80
70
60
50
40
30
20
10
0

THE BEST PART OF TODAY WAS:

THANK YOU FOR ALL THE AMAZING THINGS IN MY LIFE!

I AM FEELING:

ANGRY SAD OK HAPPY EXCITED SILLY

/ /

DATE

The world is amazing.

TODAY I AM GRATEFUL FOR:

MY HAPPINESS SCALE

100
90
80
70
60
50
40
30
20
10
0

I AM FEELING:

ANGRY SAD OK HAPPY EXCITED SILLY

THANK YOU FOR ALL THE AMAZING THINGS IN MY LIFE!

Today I am a leader.

/ /

DATE

SOMETHING AWESOME THAT HAPPENED:

TODAY I AM GRATEFUL FOR:

MY
HAPPINESS
SCALE

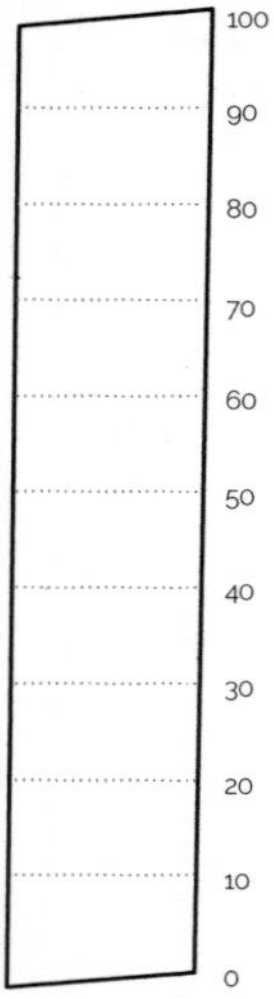

THANK YOU
FOR ALL THE
AMAZING
THINGS IN
MY LIFE!

I AM FEELING:

ANGRY SAD OK HAPPY EXCITED SILLY